Teach Me About Potty Training

Written by Joy Berry
Illustrated by Dana Regan

Copyright © 2008 by Joy Berry

Every person goes peepee.

Every person goes poopoo.

I go peepee and poopoo too.

Sometimes I go peepee and poopoo in my pants.

My pants get wet and dirty.

When my pants get wet and dirty, it smells bad.

I feel uncomfortable wearing wet and dirty pants.

I do not like to go peepee and poopoo in my pants.

Other people do not like it when I go peepee and poopoo in my pants.

There is a special thing in which I can go peepee and poopoo.

It is called a toilet.

I am careful around the toilet.

The toilet is in the bathroom.

Bathrooms away from home are often called restrooms.

There is a restroom almost everywhere I go.

There are restrooms in stores, restaurants, gas stations, and parks.

There are restrooms in schools, libraries, and theaters.

There is always a toilet for me to use in every restroom.

The toilet makes a loud noise when I flush it.

The noise scares me.

I tell someone that the noise scares me.

That person lets me flush the toilet over and over again.

I get used to the sound.

It does not scare me anymore.

I am scared that I might fall into the toilet.

I tell someone that I am scared.

That person shows me how to sit on the toilet.

I lean forward and hold on with both hands so that I will feel safe.

I put toilet paper into the toilet bowl.

I flush it.

The toilet paper goes away and does not come back.

That scares me.

It makes me wonder if the toilet might take me away, too.

I tell someone that I am scared that the toilet might take me away.

That person shows me the hole inside the toilet.

I see that it is too small for me to fit through.

I see that the toilet cannot take me away, and I feel better.

I watch other people use the toilet.

I see that boys stand up when they go peepee.

They face the toilet, lift the seat, and peepee into the toilet bowl.

I see that girls sit down when they go peepee.

They sit on the toilet seat and peepee into the toilet bowl.

I see that both boys and girls sit down when they go poopoo.

They sit on the toilet seat and poopoo into the toilet bowl.

If I am not tall enough to use the toilet, I can go peepee and poopoo into a pottychair.

I ask someone to help me dump the peepee and poopoo into the toilet.

Sometimes I need help to go peepee and poopoo.

I need someone to help me take my pants down.

I need someone to help me pull them up.

After I use the toilet, I wipe my bottom with toilet paper.

I put the dirty toilet paper into the toilet bowl.

I flush the toilet.

I wash my hands.

I feel good that I did not go peepee and poopoo in my pants.

Potty Training Song Lyrics

A Toilet is Not Scary
Track 2 & 3

A toilet is not scary.
A toilet is okay.
It won't bite you,
And it won't hurt you,
And it won't take you away.

If you feel you need to,
Here's what you can do.
Use the toilet.
Remember to flush it.
It will be good for you.

I Know How to Use the Potty
Track 4 & 5

I know how to use the potty.
I really know my stuff.
I know how to use the potty,
Cause now I'm big enough.

No more diapers.
No more wet pants.
No more icky poo.
No more tears,
And no more fears,
Cause I know what to do.

I know how to use the potty.
I really know my stuff.
I know how to use the potty,
Cause now I'm big enough.

Copyright © Joy Berry, 2020
Reprinted by permission. Originally Published 2008

The statements and opinions expressed in this work are solely those of the author and do not reflect the thoughts or opinions of the publisher.

Every effort has been made to trace the copyright holder(s) and obtain permission to reproduce all elements of this material.

All rights reserved. No part of this book may be reproduced or used in any manner without the prior written permission of the copyright owner, except for the use of brief quotations in a book review. For inquiries or to request permission, contact the publisher at rights@lemurpress.com

ISBN 978-1-63617-038-1

Published by Lemur Press
lemurpress.com

LEMUR PRESS